JOSEPH'S AMAZING COAT

by Teddy Slater

Little
Shepherd™
BOOKS

an imprint of

SCHOLASTIC INC.

New York   Toronto   London   Auckland   Sydney
Mexico City   New Delhi   Hong Kong   Buenos Aires

ISBN 0-439-81509-6

© 2006 Scholastic Inc.

ABS logo trademark and copyright American Bible Society,
1865 Broadway, New York, NY 10023.

12 11 10 9 8 7 6 5 4 3 2 1   6 7 8 9 10 11/0

Illustrations by Duendes del Sur
Designed by Joan Moloney

Printed in the U.S.A.
First printing, February 2006

EDUCATOR'S NOTE

Dear Parents,

Welcome to the Scholastic Read and Learn Reader series. We have taken more than 80 years of experience with teachers, parents, and children and put it into a program that is designed to match your child's interests and skills.

- Look at the book together. Encourage your child to read the title and make a prediction about the story.

- Read the book together. Encourage your child to sound out words when appropriate. When your child struggles, you can help by providing the word.

- Encourage your child to retell the story. This is a great way to check for comprehension.

Scholastic Readers are designed to support your child's efforts to learn how to read at every age and every stage. Enjoy helping your child learn to read and love to read.

—*Francie Alexander*
Chief Education Officer
Scholastic Education

Jacob lived in the land of Canaan.
He had twelve sons. One of his sons
was named Joseph.

Of all his sons, Jacob loved Joseph best.

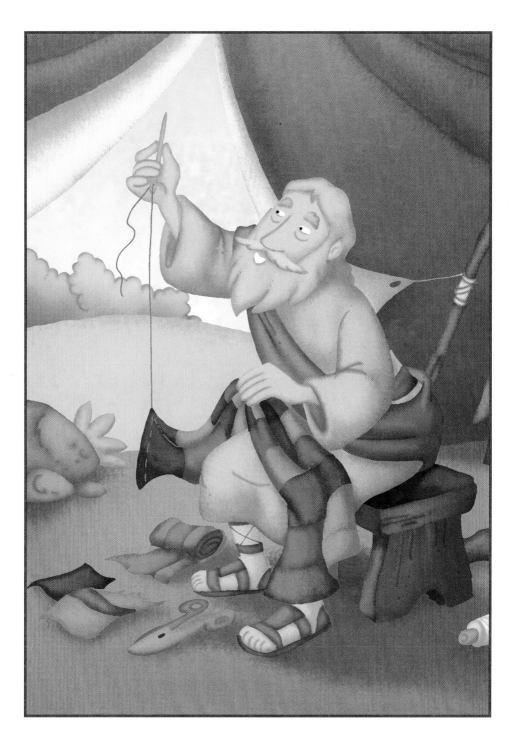

When Joseph was seventeen, Jacob made a fancy coat for him.

Joseph's brothers were jealous. They would not speak a kind word to him.

One night, Joseph dreamed that he and his brothers each had a bundle of wheat. Joseph's bundle stood up and the others bowed down to it.

Joseph also dreamed that the sun and moon and eleven stars bowed down to him.

Joseph's dreams made his brothers angry. "Do you really think you are going to rule over us?" they asked.

One day, the brothers were working
in the fields. They saw Joseph coming.
"Here comes that dreamer," said Levi.
"Let's teach him a lesson."

Joseph's brothers tore off his fancy coat.
Then they threw him into a deep pit.

Soon some traders came along. They were on their way to Egypt.

The brothers sold Joseph to the traders for twenty pieces of silver.

The traders put Joseph in chains. They took him to Egypt to be a slave.

Joseph's brothers rubbed goat's blood all over Joseph's coat.

They took the coat home and showed it to their father.

Jacob wept and tore his clothes. He thought his favorite son was dead.

But Joseph was alive.
The traders had sold him to a rich family
in Egypt.

With God's help, Joseph became rich, too.
In time, Joseph was almost as powerful as
Pharaoh.

God gave Joseph a special gift. He could
see the future through dreams. Pharaoh
had two strange dreams. He told them to
Joseph.

In the first dream, seven thin ears of grain swallowed seven fat ears of grain. In the second dream, seven skinny cows ate seven fat ones.

Joseph told Pharaoh what the dreams meant.

In seven years, the rain would stop falling. The crops would stop growing.

Pharaoh believed Joseph.

He told his people to save some of their grain.

In seven years, they would need it.

Joseph was right.

Seven years later, the rain stopped falling.
The grain stopped growing.

Thanks to Joseph, the Egyptians still had food.

But people from other lands had none.

A hungry family from the land of Canaan came to Egypt.

They bowed down to Joseph. The men were his brothers!

The dreams Joseph had when he was seventeen had come true.

The brothers were afraid that Joseph would punish them.

But Joseph was not angry. "God brought me here to save lives," he said.

Joseph sent for his father. Jacob and his sons made their home in the land of Goshen.

Jacob's children all had many children.

They became the Twelve Tribes of Israel.

Do you know . . .

. . . that Jacob (page 4) was also called "Israel"?

. . . that Canaan (page 4) was also called ancient Palestine? It was located between the Jordan River, the Dead Sea, and the Mediterranean.

. . . that in those days only rich people could afford a coat (page 7)? A coat was very special.

. . . that traders (page 15) often used camels to carry goods over long distances? Camels can travel much farther and need less water than donkeys.

. . . that Pharaoh (page 21) was the name the ancient Egyptians used for their ruler?

. . . that the Twelve Tribes of Israel (page 31) were named after Joseph's brothers and his sons?